W9-BWT-980

Cape Breton

Cape Breton

Photographs by Owen Fitzgerald

Introduction by
Robert J. Morgan

Toronto
OXFORD UNIVERSITY PRESS
1978

To Mom and Dad and Joyce

My thanks are due to Larry Bonner, Bob Brooks, Fr. Donnie Campbell, Parker Donham, Raymond Fahey, June and Robert Frank, Al Gilbert, Fred Guy, David Heath, Ray Ivony, Robert MacDonald, Eric MacEwan, Donnie MacIssac, Angus MacKillop, The Hon. Vince MacLean, Russell MacLellan, Terry MacLellan, Joe MacMullen, Ian MacNeil, John McPhee, Mr & Mrs Leslie Morley, and Freeman Patterson, for all their help and encouragement. I am especially grateful to Bob Morgan for writing the introduction to this book.   OF

Canadian Cataloguing in Publication Data
Fitzgerald, Owen
Cape Breton

ISBN 0-19-540295-2

1. Cape Breton Island, N.S. — Description and travel — Views.   I. Title.

FC2343.4.F58   917.16 '9 '00222   C78-001365-4
F1039.C2F58

©Oxford University Press (Canadian Branch) 1978
ISBN 0-19-540295-2
1 2 3 4-1 0 9 8
Printed in Hong Kong by
EVERBEST PRINTING COMPANY LIMITED

The Love of Cape Breton

Years ago a Cape Bretoner, Dan Alex MacDonald, composed a Gaelic song in honour of his beloved island. It began 'Se Ceap Breatainn tir mo ghraidh':

Cape Breton, the land of my love,
Is a land of trees and lofty mountains.
Cape Breton is the land of my love;
The fairest land on earth.

Dan Alex expressed the private love of all Cape Bretoners for this island. For the soaring seascapes of the Cabot Trail ('down north' to Cape Bretoners); the crashing waves at Louisbourg; the neat simplicity of Baddeck; the crisp white ice against the blue of the Bras d'Or Lakes at spring break-up — for the haunting beauty that excites the blood of Cape Bretoners no matter how far they are from home.

But the love of Cape Breton is far more than the love of the land. Living away, Cape Bretoners long for the smell of the coal stacks, the flare in the sky as the metal is poured at the steel plant, the cooking-cabbage smell of the pulp mill, the delicious sound of the pipes and fiddles at the outdoor concerts. All are reminders of childhood, of friendships, of home.

This is no gentle island. It is rugged, a country of wind and perverse weather changes where a soft, clear day can turn into a damp, bitter one. Nevertheless, seventeenth-century fishermen from Spain, Portugal, France, and England found shelter in the island's Atlantic harbours.

Its history has often been cruel. The Scots actually attempted a settlement at Baleine, only to be expelled by the French. Nicolas Denys established a trading post, only to be attacked by jealous fellow-countrymen.

Then came Louisbourg, France's last great stronghold on the Atlantic coast. Despite poor soil, Atlantic gales, and isolation, France made Louisbourg a keystone in the trade of its empire. The Fortress protected French traders, fishermen, and citizens. Isle-Royale, as the French called Cape Breton, flourished until all was destroyed when the Fortress fell to the British, first in 1745 and finally in 1758.

The island was almost abandoned until Loyalist arrivals, fleeing the American Revolution, convinced the British Crown to establish Cape Breton as a separate colony in 1784. The Acadian French who had stayed in the island, despite the Expulsion of 1758, were joined by others returned from exile. Scots and Irish immigrants followed. In the course of time the Scots have made Cape Breton a centre of Gaelic culture in Canada. Here the Gaelic is still spoken and the pipes, the fiddle, and the stepdance will flourish forever.

In 1820 Cape Breton was 'annexed' to Nova Scotia, but the island retained its psychological independence. Mines opened, producing coal for fuel and shipping; they grew, and in 1900 a steel plant was built at Sydney. Cape Bretoners became the only people in the Maritime Provinces whose lives were involved in heavy industry. Coal, steel, unions, strikes, Communism, Socialism—these are alien words to people east of Montreal, but not to Cape Bretoners.

Then the coal was no longer needed; then the steel plant was about to close. There was unemployment and fear. But the 'Capers' stayed — they are going to save the steel plant, and the mines are opening again.

So if the history is cruel, Cape Bretoners persist. Tough, stubborn, determined, outspoken, clannish, proud, they reflect the island's ruggedness: its rocky hills, bold coastline, steep valleys, and majestic scenery.

But the greatest gift that this island has given them is the one that is most elusive to Canadians: the gift of identity. Cape Bretoners know who they are. They have struggled through adversity and are deeply imbued with the island's culture—that beautiful mixture of Scottish and Irish, Micmac and Acadian. They enjoy Cape Breton music, Cape Breton dancing, 'good Cape Breton tea'—or rum—and speak with a gentle Cape Breton lilt.

Owen Fitzgerald's photographs are one Cape Bretoner's tribute to his homeland, an attempt to capture some of this island's beauty and mood and to portray a few of its people. May they help you to understand why we love 'an innis aigh' — this happy island.

ROBERT J. MORGAN

Sydney, Cape Breton
April 1978

1   A foggy day at Lighthouse Point.

2 Chéticamp River near its source in the Cape Breton Highlands.

3 *(right)* Cabot Trail winding around Cap Rouge.

4 The water's edge.

5 Flint Island.

6 *Bluenose II* in Sydney Harbour.

7 Gathering seaweed at Chéticamp.

8 Ship-building at l'Ardoise.

9   Lobster traps piled up in New Haven harbour.

10 Painting a boat at Englishtown.

11   Off Money Point near Cape North.

12   Lobster fisherman with buoys at
Glace Bay.

13   *(right)* Setting out for lobster in
Pleasant Bay.

14   On the beach at Pondville,
Isle Madame.

15 Young girls at the Gaelic Mod,
St Ann's.

16 Dancers waiting to perform at the Gaelic Mod.

17 (right) Dancing at the Gaelic Mod.

18 Drummer boy at the
Sydney Scottish Tattoo.

19   In the pond at Pondville,
Isle Madame.

20 Funfair at the Cape Breton Farmers' Exhibition, North Sydney.

21 Horse and rider at the Farmers' Exhibition.

22 Mimes at the Tarbot Music
Festival.

23 *(right) Rise and Follies of Cape
Breton Island:* the Steel City Players.

24 Glendale Fiddle Festival.

25   A quiet listener at the
Tarbot Music Festival.

26 Lee Cremo, one of the world's great fiddlers, at the Tarbot Music Festival.

27 Deannie Munroe Beaton, piper in the Cape Breton tartan, Tarbot Music Festival.

28   The church at Bay St Lawrence.

29　Day's end at Framboise.

30   Spring in the woods at
Pleasant Bay.

31   *(right)* Fishing for salmon on the
Margaree River.

32   Official opening of the Cossit House, Sydney, September 1977.

33   *(right)* 'Beinn Bhreagh' (Beautiful Mountain), the summer home of Alexander Graham Bell, overlooking Baddeck.

34 Abandoned farmhouse near Iona,
on the Barra Strait.

35 *(right)* Inside the Savoy Theatre,
Glace Bay.

36 St Peter's Church, Chéticamp,
built in 1893.

37 · Interior of St Peter's, Chéticamp.

38 Mr Sampson of L'Ardoise, chopping wood.

39 (right) Sysco steel plant, Sydney.

40   Miners coming up at Number 26 Colliery, Glace Bay.

41   *(right)* 'Men of the Deeps', the miners' choir at the Tarbot Music Festival.

42   Coal-drilling ship off Port Morien.

43 On board the coal driller.

44   Pouring at the Sydney steel plant.

45 Heavy-water plant, Glace Bay.

46 *(left)* Deep in the woods near Pleasant Bay.

47 Albert Bridge on the Mira River.

48 Mabou Highlands and the
Northumberland Strait
at Sight Point.

49 Mary Ann Falls between Ingonish
and Neil's Harbour.

50 Maple leaves in the fall.

51 *(right)* Fortress Louisbourg, seen from across the marshes.

52 Citadel Guardhouse, Louisbourg.

53 Guard inside the entrance of the King's Bastion, Louisbourg.

54   A cold and windy day on
Rue Toulouse, Louisbourg.

55 Dozing in the shelter of the Guardhouse, Louisbourg.

56   King's Bastion Barracks, dry moat
and palisade, Louisbourg.

57 Soldier at a window, Louisbourg.

58 The Chapel, Louisbourg.

59 A quiet moment in which to draw,
Louisbourg.

60 *(left)* Excavations, Louisbourg.

61 Visiting the poultry-yard, Louisbourg.

62 *(left)* Winter over the town of Louisbourg.

63 Houses in snow, Louisbourg.

64 (left) Cannon on the ramparts,
Louisbourg.

65 Snow fills the moat of Louisbourg
and blows around the Bastion's walls.

66 Keltic Lodge, on Middle Head promontory, north of Ingonish Beach.

67 Winter near Grand Lac, south of Chéticamp. The barn is attached to the farmhouse
for warmth, accessibility, and strength in the wind.

68 Lighthouse in drift ice on Bras d'Or, below the Seal Island bridge.

69 St Michael's Church, Baddeck.

70 Baddeck lighthouse seen from the entrance to the museum of the Alexander Graham Bell National Historic Park.

71   Baddeck in winter seen from Government Wharf.

72 Ice fishing on the Mira River.

73 *(right)* Sheep wintering at Margaree.

74 Looking up the frozen coast towards Chéticamp from Margaree Harbour.

75 *(right)* A stream in the Margaree Valley.

76 Neil's Harbour.

77 *(right)* Cap Rouge on the Cabot Trail looking south.

78   Barn at Middle River, just off
the Cabot Trail.

79 Lighthouse at Louisbourg.

80　Fishing village at Havenside.

81 Southwest shoreline of Bras d'Or at Johnstown.

82   Chéticamp River in July.

83 Fishing at l'Ardoise.

84 Loch Lomond.

85 St Lawrence Bay on the Northern-
most coast of the Island.

86 (*left*) Sunset at Chéticamp.

87 Rocky beach at Ingonish harbour.

88 Running from the waves.